God, Ge...

Gay Christians

Acts 15 and Change in the Church

Andrew Goddard

Lecturer in Christian Ethics, Wycliffe Hall, Oxford

GROVE BOOKS LIMITED
RIDLEY HALL RD CAMBRIDGE CB3 9HU

Contents

Acknowledgments

Many people and groups have helped me deepen my understanding as I have studied the difficult subject of homosexuality in recent years. The particular focus of this booklet on Acts 15 arose in part from involvement with the Oxford Diocesan Sexuality Group and its discussions. The ideas were originally presented as a lecture at the Oxford University Summer School for students working for the Masters in Applied Theology degree. This was subsequently discussed in a seminar with a number of fellow tutors (Graham Tomlin, David Wenham and Jeremy Duff) at Wycliffe Hall and read by a number of fellow members of the Grove Ethics Group. I am grateful for their responses and dialogue which helped me clarify and correct my thinking and sharpen the argument. The confusions and errors which remain and the views expressed are, of course, mine and not theirs.

The Cover Illustration is by Peter Ashton

First Impression April 2001
ISSN 1740-854X
ISBN 1 85174 461 4

1
Introduction

The nature and moral status of homosexual relationships, the church's response to gay Christians, and its traditional condemnation of all homosexual acts is for many people one of the most significant ethical issues facing the Christian church at the start of the 21st century. Although some of this focus and emphasis must be questioned, even repented of, it cannot be dismissed.[1] The reason this discussion has gained such significance and arouses such strong passions is that, rightly or wrongly, it has been seen as a test in three central and interconnected areas—the church's prophetic witness, its pastoral responsibility and its political identity.

In relation to the church's prophetic witness, the question it raises is how the church today is faithful to the Word of God in Scripture. Must it be seen to uphold its traditional understanding of biblical teaching in the face of the secularization and sexualization of society or must it instead bear witness to the inclusivity of the gospel in the light of the historic rejection of gay people by both church and society? Correlated with this is the church's pastoral responsibility. Many now recognize that the church has often failed to show Christ's love and provide pastoral care for those who feel strong attraction to fellow members of the same sex. How then, in relation to gay Christians, should the church speak and live the truth in love? Thirdly, the spectrum of answers to these questions means this issue has become highly political and threatens the unity of God's people. The Bishop of Oxford (who chairs the Sexuality Group in the House of Bishops) opens his most recent paper on the issue with the sentence, 'The status of same sex relationships is the most divisive issue now facing the Church of England, indeed the whole Anglican Communion and many other churches as well.'[2]

Unfortunately, much of the popular and media debate rarely gets beyond polemic and confrontation between 'revisionists' who seek a wholesale rethink of traditional church teaching and 'traditionalists' wishing to defend the church's historic negative judgment on homosexuality. More substantial documents have, however, been produced by many British denominations

---

1 'That the issue should have become so highly dramatized calls for repentance on the part of all members of the church. It suggests that the gospel has not been directing the acts, words and thoughts of Christians on this subject.' 'St Andrew's Day Statement' in Timothy Bradshaw (ed), *The Way Forward?* (London: Hodder and Stoughton, 1997) pp 5–6. Online at http://www.episcopalian. org/cclec/paper-st-andrews-day.html
2 Richard Harries, 'Same Sex Relationships—The Unresolved Questions.' Available at http://www. oxford.anglican.org/bishop/

in recent years[3] and the scholarly literature on the subject is massive. It is clear that if a way forward is to be found for the church it will require engagement with a wide range of issues—the experience of gay Christians, the nature of human sexuality and marriage, how we live together in a church where there are serious moral disagreements over the right response to our changing cultural context.[4] However, central to the debate will be the exegesis and application of Scripture. The tendency, on both sides, has been to focus on the few biblical passages which prohibit or speak negatively of homosexual conduct.[5] Although of vital importance these can no longer be the sole focus in discussion of how Scripture bears on our current deliberations. In recent years, another biblical passage and theme has begun to appear in the debates: the narrative of the Jerusalem Council in Acts 15 and the inclusion of the Gentiles by the early Jewish church.[6]

Although this approach may initially appear to have little or no value for discussion of homosexuality, in the light of the three crucial issues noted above, its potential importance is much clearer. In the early church the response to Gentiles who wished to follow Jesus also raised important prophetic, pastoral and political concerns. It too was seen by many to threaten truth, love and unity among God's people. The apostolic church had to discern whether the welcome of Gentiles into the historic people of God was a faithful action in accordance with truth and what requirements should be made on non-Jewish followers of Jesus. There was a recognition that any response had to demonstrate the love and welcome of Christ towards those traditionally excluded from God's people. Finally, the issue had the potential to divide the infant church and destroy the unity of the Spirit.

In this light, our different context and debate may be illuminated by the early church's response to Gentiles on at least two levels. Firstly, we may find guidance as to how, as the body of Christ, we should deliberate on contentious issues and in particular how Scripture and experience of the Spirit

---

3   The Church of England Bishops produced *Issues in Human Sexuality* in 1991 and in 1995 Cardinal Hume issued a note on church teaching concerning homosexual people (http://www.bway.net/ ~halsall/lgbh/lgbh-humegays.html). The Methodist Conference has debated the issue on a number of occasions, the URC published a study in 1999 (http://www.urc.org.uk/human_sexuality) and the Baptist Union launched a new study guide ('Making Moral Choices in our Relationships') at its assembly in 2000.

4   For recent British discussion across the spectrum of views see Michael Vasey, *Strangers and Friends* (London: Hodder and Stoughton, 1995) and Dave Leal, *Debating Homosexuality* (Grove Ethical booklet E 101). Tim Bradshaw (ed), *op cit* remains the best single volume and the editor's concluding chapter is online at http://fifamerica.faithweb.com/ARTICLES/OCTOBER1999/Art31.htm.

5   For an introduction to these see Mark Bonnington and Bob Fyall, *Homosexuality and the Bible* (Grove Biblical booklet B 1).

6   Among those drawing attention to this are two contributors to Blackwells' *Challenges in Contemporary Theology* series—Stephen Fowl, *Engaging Scripture: A Model for Theological Interpretation* (Oxford: Blackwells, 1998) pp 119–27; Eugene Rogers, *Sexuality and the Christian Body: Their Way into the Triune God* (Oxford: Blackwells, 1999) ch 2. Other important scholars referring to this passage in the debate and discussed below are J Siker and Luke T Johnson.

may be brought into such discussions. Secondly, and more controversially, a number of 'revisionist' writers have argued that there are illuminating parallels between the inclusion of Gentile believers into the early church and the call for gay Christians to be fully welcomed and their relationships affirmed by the church today. This decision of the early church and the text of Acts 15 may therefore appear to challenge the 'traditionalist' monopoly on scriptural texts in the debate.

This scholarly debate is now beginning to appear in the ecclesial discussion. Bishop Richard Harries, after a brief discussion of different interpretations of the classic texts, makes the following observation:

The way the early church admitted Gentiles also, it is argued, offers a precedent for us today. The first Christians, who were Jewish, saw the Holy Spirit clearly at work in Gentiles and as a result came to the conclusion that they could be baptized as Christians without first having to be circumcised and without keeping the Jewish law. The clear teaching of the Old Testament about ritual purity and food laws, for example, was set aside. On the basis of mutual friendship within the Christian community today it has been argued that we might be able to see the Holy Spirit at work in loving same-sex relationships and as a consequence gay and lesbian people in such relationships should be warmly welcomed and fully affirmed.[7]

Within this broader context this booklet's aim is limited. It seeks to examine this new biblically-based claim and test how valuable Acts 15 might be for both the structure and the substance of the current homosexuality debate. In particular, it questions whether the passage and the early church experience to which it bears witness can be used to draw 'revisionist' conclusions.

The next chapter offers a brief summary of the context and content of Acts 15 and the early church debate. It then outlines the hermeneutical problems some will have with *any* normative appeal to this text in contemporary church discussions. Chapter three turns to what value the passage might have in guiding the church as it seeks to interpret Scripture, discern the work of God today, and maintain truth, love and unity while living with its disagreements over homosexuality. The main section—chapter four—then explores the strengths and weaknesses of the analogy suggested between Gentile Christians and gay Christians, mapping what possible responses might arise from using Acts 15 as a paradigm in our current disagreements over homosexual relationships. Finally, some conclusions are drawn about the 'revisionist' case and how Acts 15 may assist in the prophetic, pastoral and political witness of the church in the homosexuality debate.

---

7   Harries, *op cit*, pp 7–8. Reference to the welcome of Gentiles is included in the rationale offered for liturgies blessing same sex unions currently proposed within New Westminster Diocese [see www.vancouver.anglican.ca].

2
Church Debate Then and Now—Can Acts 15 Help?

Luke's account of the Jerusalem Council in Acts 15 has attracted a great deal of attention from critical New Testament scholarship. The questions it raises from such a perspective are numerous—the historicity and sources of Luke's narrative, its relationship to Paul's story in Galatians and the Antioch dispute recorded there, the interesting textual variants in different manuscripts. They are also of minimal value for anyone interested in preaching, practical and pastoral theology, or the use of the Bible in ethics. The scholarly focus on them is, in many ways, an indictment of much mainstream biblical criticism.[8] Rather than examining the classical critical questions, the remainder of this section treats the text as a narrative whole before addressing hermeneutical issues.

Acts 15 must be read as part of a much wider and central narrative in Luke's account. This begins with Peter's call to preach the gospel to the Gentile Cornelius which leads to Cornelius' conversion and some subsequent controversy (Acts 10–11). Luke then reports on Paul's missionary work among Gentiles with its base in Antioch (Acts 13–14), showing that a radical new step has taken place in the community of Jesus' disciples. Gentiles, traditionally excluded from God's chosen people, are now being welcomed into this new community as full members of the people of God without becoming circumcised Jews.

In Acts 15 we discover that, unsurprisingly, this break with tradition met with a strong hostile reaction from some Jewish believers in Jesus. They are insistent that Gentiles cannot be saved unless they are circumcised (v 1). As a result Luke frankly confesses there was dissension and dispute within the church (v 2). Paul and Barnabas therefore head to Jerusalem—the mother church—in order to seek a resolution to this conflict. They enthusiastically report what they have seen God doing in their mission to Gentiles. Other believers are, however, emphatic that 'The Gentiles must be circumcised and required to obey the law of Moses' (v 5). Although we do not know the arguments advanced for such a view, in addition to the well-established traditions within Judaism of what was expected of Gentile proselytes, texts such as Gen 17, Is 2 and Is 42.4 would likely have been appealed to in order to justify this position.

Once the issues have been laid before the assembly, the leaders consider how to proceed and what to require of new Gentile converts. Luke offers

---

8   See the comments in Luke T Johnson, *Scripture and Discernment: Decision Making in the Church* (Nashville: Abingdon Press, 1996) pp 70, 71. The earlier edition of this work appeared in 1983.

edited highlights of what was clearly a lengthy and serious discussion (v 7). Peter's contribution is recorded most fully (vv 7–11). Peter speaks first and foremost of God's call on his life to preach the gospel to Gentiles. He affirms God's acceptance of Gentiles, demonstrated by his gift of the Holy Spirit to them and their purification by faith. He rebukes those who are questioning this and adding conditions with the memorable and shocking question— 'Why do you try to test God by putting on the necks of the disciples a yoke that neither we nor our fathers have been able to bear?' Peter is then followed by the testimony of Paul and Barnabas who likewise appeal to their experience of God at work through them among the Gentiles (v 12).

James, the brother of Jesus, then speaks and proposes how to proceed. He refers to Peter's testimony of God's work and, in the first reference to Scripture recorded in the dispute, cites a biblical text supporting Peter's experience. This comes from the Greek Old Testament of Amos 9 but with other prophetic passages echoed or alluded to in the citation. James' judgment is then given—stop harassing or troubling Gentile converts and make only limited requirements of them (*not* circumcision). This judgment, from someone probably expected to be cautious if not hostile about radical change, receives general approval. It is then relayed to the Gentile believers in a personally delivered letter which describes the Council's final decision in the momentous phrase, 'It seemed good to the Holy Spirit and to us' (v 28).

Precedent and Objections

It is important to acknowledge from the outset that no broader theological conclusions or wider ecclesiological lessons are explicitly drawn by Luke from this narrative. He does not tell this story to illustrate or justify wider counsel to his readers. He simply offers a description of how the early church came to welcome Gentiles and the grounds on which they did this. The first hurdle that must therefore be overcome by any Christian appeal to Acts 15 today is whether it is even legitimate to use the experience surrounding the Jerusalem Council as in any sense a norm or guide for contemporary church disputes. The arguments between Christians caused by appeals to narratives of Christian initiation in Acts (particularly the experience of Spirit-baptism) highlight the difficulties in taking Luke's account as paradigmatic or drawing out universal principles from particular incidents in the apostolic church.[9]

The account in Acts 15 has, however, been appealed to during recent church debates over women's ordination and so its use in relation to homosexuality is not in itself an original hermeneutical argument. In particular,

---

9 See, for example, the discussion of Luke-Acts in Max Turner, *Baptism in the Holy Spirit* (Grove Renewal booklet R 2).

the evangelical New Testament scholar and former Principal of Wycliffe Hall, Dr Dick France, preached a sermon in March 1994 which appealed to Acts 15 in defending his own change of mind to accept women in church leadership. Using v 28 cited above he argued that the decision to include Gentiles seemed 'to offer interesting parallels to the present issue' of women's ordination.[10] In response, some evangelicals who opposed France highlighted their un-happiness with this analogy and raised three central concerns which, if ac-cepted, would invalidate arguments for change based on this text.[11]

First, it has been claimed that Luke's concern here is not with the broad issue of how the church should live but the specific, indeed unique, experi-ence of the entrance of Gentiles into God's people. This was a once-for-all momentous work of God's grace to which Luke bears witness as he tells of the transition from Jewish renewal movement to world-wide church. We therefore cannot use his account of how God guided the church in this in-stance as a basis for changing church doctrine and practice today. Secondly, and related, Luke places great emphasis on apostolic authority and experi-ence (particularly that of Peter) in his account and it is claimed that apostolic authority is mediated to us today by the New Testament and not by leaders within the church or claimed contemporary experiences of the Spirit. Thirdly, Luke is showing how the church came to a fuller realization of the work of God in Christ. This discernment and unpacking of the meaning of the gos-pel is fundamentally different from any claim to have gained some new rev-elation or insight into an issue of ethics or church order through contemporary experience or new knowledge.

Responses to the Objections

These are important concerns which may lead some to reject any use of Acts 15 in relation to contentious issues in the church today. They are not, however, conclusive. If similar arguments were applied consistently they would run the risk of preventing any Scripture guiding us as we face new situations of controversy and division within the church.

First, while Luke's primary goal is to give an account and justification of the incorporation of uncircumcised Gentiles into God's people, it would be wrong to conclude that legitimate use of the text is now limited to a lesson in church history or historical theology. In order to gain benefit from Acts 15 for the contemporary church it is possible to clarify and classify the particu-lar conflict recounted there, imaginatively discern analogous situations to-day, and then draw lessons from Luke's account. This pattern of interpretation is regularly used in appealing to Scripture and, if developed carefully, can

---

10 'It seemed good to the Holy Spirit and us,' *Churchman*, Vol 108 No 3 (1994), p 235.
11 For example, Melvin Tinker's response to France, *ibid*, pp 242–6.

be of great value. Although Acts 15 could be appealed to for any disagreement or division within the Christian community it is probably better to be more specific. Acts 15 acts best as a paradigm today in situations where there is a well-established traditional majority view within the people of God but this view (although it claims to have God's authority—especially through his Word) is now being questioned by a significant group within the faith community. Viewed as an instance of this wider category, the early church debate about whether and on what basis Gentiles might become full members of God's people can shed fresh biblical light on how the church might respond in a number of contentious areas including homosexuality.

The second claim—the uniqueness of the apostles—can similarly be overplayed. Clearly the church must remain under apostolic biblical authority and can never claim equivalent authority for any of its own decisions to revise its traditional teaching and practice. However, just as Christians are learning how to read the Bible biblically through study of how the prophets and apostles read and interpreted earlier Scripture, so apostolic approaches to resolving disputes should be able to guide the church today.

Finally, although the nature of doctrinal and ethical development is complex and controversial, if we truly believe the church is to be *semper reformanda* then it needs to be open to correction by God's Word and Spirit. The narrative Luke provides of such correction in relation to Jewish attitudes to Gentiles provides an excellent biblical foundation for understanding how such reform may be brought about by God today in other areas.[12]

Despite the difficulties and dangers, therefore, the task of relating Acts 15 to current debates is not wholly illegitimate. We must now turn to the two areas noted earlier as parallels between Acts 15 and the homosexuality debate—the methodological issues of style and structure and the more specific issue of substance in the two debates. The next chapter asks what general lessons we might learn from Luke's account when dealing with conflict and disagreement within the church. Chapter four then explores whether more substantial analogies can legitimately be drawn between the early church response to Gentiles and the contemporary church's relationship with gay Christians.

---

12 David Wright, 'The Homosexuality Debate and the Reform of the Church,' *Anvil*, Vol 15, No 1 (1998) pp 22–33 is an excellent discussion of this theme.

3

Ethics and Hermeneutics
in a Divided Church—Acts 15 as a Paradigm?

This shorter chapter highlights five general lessons drawn from Luke's narrative that show how Christians should act in situations where the church finds its traditional stance being questioned from within. These may give important procedural guidance as to how the church should conduct both its current debates on homosexual relationships and other ethical disagreements more widely.[13]

First, and most obviously, major disagreement and disputes within the church about how to act are not unusual nor are they always to be taken as a sign of serious apostasy or culpable error (although Gal 2 reminds us they may be). As Luke Johnson comments:

> Luke clearly sees conflict and debate as legitimate and perhaps even necessary elements in the process of discernment...Luke is unembarrassed by it, for such disagreement serves to reveal the true bases for fellowship, and elicit the fundamental principles of community identity.[14]

Secondly, when there is such disagreement, Christians who hold differing views need to meet together, to listen to each other, and to discern God's will in such a way that the unity of the church is maintained with minimal damage to its *koinonia*. This, clearly, is the underlying rationale to the convening of what we know as the Jerusalem Council.

Thirdly, Christians must be open to God working in surprising ways which challenge well-established and cherished beliefs and practices. Although this is seen to a certain extent in Acts 15 it is conveyed most clearly in Luke's preceding narrative of Peter's response to God's call to preach the gospel to the Gentile Cornelius.

Fourthly, the Council gives pride of place to the testimony and witness of those who have been at the forefront of the church's mission and engagement with the issue under discussion. It is their account of what they have discovered about God's contemporary work which is so important in the decision-making process. This procedure began back in Acts 11 where Pe-

---

13 Rowan Williams' 'Making moral decisions' in Robin Gill (ed), *Cambridge Companion to Christian Ethics* (Cambridge: CUP, 2001) pp 3–15 includes a thought-provoking discussion of moral discernment in the church originally given at the Lambeth Conference.
14 Luke Johnson, *The Acts of the Apostles* (Minnesota: Liturgical Press, 1992) p 271.

ter's testimony won round sceptics. It is repeated and confirmed in Jerusalem. Johnson again comments,

> Priority is given to the narratives of faith, for it is such narratives which enable private religious experience to reach the level of public discernment ...Peter does not appear as the judge but another witness...Paul and Barnabas do not appear as advocates pleading a case but as simple witnesses ...Such narratives open up the possibility of perceiving God working in unexpected ways.[15]

Fifthly, these narratives of experience cannot be conclusive. When the church has to decide on its response and how it should act, any decision needs to correlate the claimed discernment of God's purposes in present experience with the scriptural witness to God's past dealings with his people. James plays the crucial role in this process although Luke's account of how he appeals to Scripture is perhaps surprising. Despite some translations, James does not state that the testimonies they have heard agree with what the Bible says. It is the other way around: the words of the prophets are found to be in agreement with what Peter and Paul have been saying. In other words, as France argued in relation to women's leadership, while all true Christian theology needs to be scriptural and all experience needs to be interpreted in the light of God's revelation, it can often be the case that a new experience of God at work in the present leads to fresh understanding of the biblical text.[16]

While there are obviously differences between the conflict and its resolution in Acts 15 and any current debates, in principle these five lessons can be applied to the current church debate over gay relationships. In particular the last two need to be stressed as it can appear that those reaching differing conclusions have failed to give due weight to one or other of these.

'Traditionalists' in the homosexuality debate often appear not to give credence to the testimony of modern-day equivalents of Peter and Paul. They have certainly not always been willing to follow their example and take radical steps themselves in relation to gay people. Stephen Fowl has drawn attention to the need to be able to read the Spirit at work in a situation if one is to read Scripture aright. He argues that one of the reasons we fail here is that we are not good at forming and nurturing the patterns of relationship and types of common life which enable us to perform this vital task. In relation to gay Christians, the nearest much of the church has got to achieving this is,

---

15 *ibid.*
16 Johnson however sets up too strong and one-sided an emphasis on current experience over Scripture. Our discernment of God's action today is inextricably related to and needs to be tested by our reading of Scripture. There must be a dialectical relationship between the two.

in the words of the 1998 Lambeth Conference resolution, to 'commit ourselves to listen to the experience of homosexual people.' This is vital and must include the full range of homosexual people and not just those who tell us what we want to hear![17] However, more than listening needs to take place. Fowl makes the following telling criticism of a similar proposal implied by Johnson's reading of Acts 15:

> Any analogous application of Acts 10–15 to issues of homosexual inclusion will need to be grounded in testimonies of 'homosexual holiness.' Johnson's comments, however, indicate that the burden of providing such testimony is on homosexual Christians. This is a departure from the testifying practices of Acts. It is crucial that Peter, Paul, and Barnabas were all circumcised Jews testifying about the work of the Spirit in the lives of uncircumcised Gentile believers…It should not, then, be the responsibility of homosexual Christians to provide 'narratives of homosexual holiness' …The onus is on other Christians who may enter (or have already entered) into friendships with homosexual Christians out of which they might offer testimony of their friends' holiness. Alternatively, it may be the case that such friendships generate calls to repentance from one friend to another … Christians have no reason to think they understand how the Holy Spirit weighs in on the issue of homosexuality until they welcome homosexuals into their homes and sit down to eat with them.[18]

If 'traditionalists' seem to be lacking in 'Peter' figures, 'revisionists' are in desperate need of someone like 'James.' Although many have sought to address the traditional prohibitionist texts of Scripture and explain why they believe they are not relevant to the current debate, there has been no serious attempt to find any textual warrant in Scripture for changing the church's teaching on homosexuality.

Intriguingly, some 'revisionists' now claim Acts 15 may be an option in the quest for a biblical foundation for their position. To assess this claim requires moving on from the procedural issue and practical lessons for doing theology in the midst of ecclesial disputation. Having examined how the early church faced this challenge to its prophetic, pastoral and political witness, the focus must now turn to the substantive issue. The question now becomes 'What would it mean for the church to respond today to gay Christians as the early church did at Jerusalem in relation to Gentile Christians?'

---

17 Richard Harries, 'More Talk than Listening' in *The Tablet*, 15th August 1998 suggests selective listening was a major problem at Lambeth.
18 Stephen Fowl, *op cit*, pp 121, 122. For a powerful example of this see Richard Hays, *The Moral Vision of the New Testament* (Edinburgh: T and T Clark, 1996) pp 379ff based on his friendship with Gary.

4
Gay Christians and Gentile Christians—
Acts 15 as Authorization of Revisionist Beliefs?

In seeking parallels between gay Christians today and Gentile Christians in the early church there are dangers of a naïve and crude parallelism whose logic, if extended, would lead to conclusions impossible to embrace. It is not sufficient to say that Gentiles were excluded on the basis of tradition and a well-established reading of Scripture but the church realized this was wrong and now it must therefore do the same in relation to gay Christians. That argument, like 'historically wrong on slavery and women, therefore wrong on homosexuality,' draws a totally unwarranted conclusion reached on other grounds. It suggests that we need to ask why the church has not been wrong in all other areas of its teaching and whether it does not therefore have to welcome and affirm all those practices it has traditionally condemned?

In drawing analogies between the debate over homosexuality and other areas it is necessary, as Jeffrey Siker argues in the most detailed exposition of this 'revisionist' argument, to demonstrate the fittingness of the proposed analogy and the legitimacy of conclusions drawn from it. Siker himself contrasts his preferred Gentile analogy to the more common alcoholic analogy, memorably summing up the concerns of many 'traditionalists' in relation to homosexuality with reference to alcoholism:

> If, instead of Alcoholics Anonymous, churches started allowing 'Drunks Divine' to organize groups in their churches (as apparently the Corinthians did!—see 1 Cor 11.21), imagine what would happen? What if practising alcoholics began arguing that their alcoholic orientation was really a gift from God and that their drunkenness was but an expression of this gift? The acceptance of such practice would be a terrible distortion of God's intentions for redeemed human communities.[19]

In order to map out and assess the potential parallels between Acts 15 and the contemporary gay debate three separate areas need to be examined—the people involved, the issue at stake, and the solution proposed.

---

19 Jeffrey S Siker, 'Homosexual Christians, the Bible and Gentile Inclusion: Confessions of a Repenting Heterosexist' in Siker (ed), *Homosexuality in the Church: Both Sides of the Debate* (Louisville: Westminster John Knox Press, 1994) p 182.

1. People Involved—Gays and Gentiles

The first and decisive question is whether or not there are good grounds to draw *any* analogy between Gentiles in the early church and gay Christians today. This issue is further complicated by the highly disputed nature of contemporary gay identity and the causes of homosexuality.[20] Whatever conclusions one draws on these debates, four parallels can be drawn between, on the one hand, first-century Gentiles and traditional Jewish (and some Jewish Christian) attitudes to them and, on the other, the contemporary gay identity and traditional Christian attitudes to homosexual people.

First, Gentiles have no say in their Gentile identity which comes to them as a given. Gay people argue that they have no say in their sexual attraction to people of the same sex which comes to them as a given.

Gentiles are such by nature [*physis*, Gal 2.15; Rom 2.14] and, although the causes of homosexual attraction remain mysterious and controversial, there is growing evidence that at least some experience of homosexual attraction may have a significant 'natural' or biological component.[21] Even if this proves not to be the case it is clear that, as with heterosexual attraction, few if any gay people consciously choose to experience homo-erotic feelings.

Secondly, Gentiles represented distinctive cultures and ways of life with which the early church had to engage. In the contemporary Western world there are gay cultures and ways of life and the church must find a response to these.

This may prove an important way of construing elements in the current church debate. It is not solely to do with the legitimacy of particular sexual acts but also how to engage a social and cultural identity. As Oliver O'Donovan has written,

> Our first and last duty in this sphere is to discern the light the gospel sheds on the gay movement of our time. The church must learn to attest

---

20 There is a long-running disagreement about both the causes of homosexuality (crudely, nature or nurture or some combination of the two) and the conceptualization of the homosexual phenomenon (essentialists versus constructionists). Essentialists holds that sexual orientations are deep and universal categories of human nature (what one author has called 'natural kinds' and thus open to scientific explanation) while constructionists hold that they are social constructs which vary across time and space. See Edward Stein, *The Mismeasure of Desire: The Science, Theory and Ethics of Sexual Orientation* (Oxford: OUP, 1999). There are important theological issues here, most fully explored by the St Andrew's Day Statement by evangelical Anglicans and responses to it in Tim Bradshaw, *The Way Forward?* especially Rowan Williams' 'Knowing Myself in Christ,' pp 12–19.

21 In the secular literature a strong argument for this is advanced by Chandler Burr in his *A Separate Creation* (London: Bantam, 1996) with further information available on his web site at http://members.aol.com/GAYGENE/index.htm. Edward Stein, *op cit*, offers a more critical approach to this research programme. Even among traditionalist Christians there is an acceptance of some biological element as in the nuanced account of Thomas Schmidt, *Straight and Narrow?* (Leicester: IVP, 1995), available from the helpful Bridges Across site at http://www.bridges-across.org/ba/science.htm. A discussion of recent surveys is found in Stanton L Jones and Mark A Yarhouse, *Homosexuality: The Use of Scientific Research in the Church's Moral Debate* (Downers Grove: IVP, 2000).

its faith in the gospel before this cultural phenomenon. The gay Christian must learn to attest the truth of the gay self-consciousness in the light of the gospel. What we commit ourselves to, when we commit ourselves to true debate, is no more and no less than this learning. But let nobody presume to announce in advance what we are going to learn before we come to learn it![22]

Thirdly, Gentiles were viewed by Jews as different, mired in immorality (especially sexual immorality), and so separated from God and under his judgment. Traditionally much of the church has viewed gay people in a similar light.[23]

This similarity lies at the heart of Siker's proposal that Gentiles rather than alcoholics are the best parallel to draw with gay people. He writes,

To be a Gentile was, in the eyes of Jews and Jewish Christians alike, the same as being a sinner, since the Gentiles did not have the law, since they were by definition unclean, polluted, and idolatrous…The crux of the analogy…lies in the observation that early Jewish Christians saw Gentiles as being sinners because they were Gentiles.[24]

Fourthly, Gentiles were kept at a distance by Jews for fear of contamination. Gay people have at times been similarly ostracized by the Christian community in its pursuit of a policy of separation and purity.

This is, of course, exactly what God challenged in Peter's life through his call to go to Cornelius (Acts 10) but it is, sadly, still the experience of many gay people in relation to the Christian church.

These four common features provide a strong basis for drawing analogies but there are also significant differences weakening any parallels. Siker himself notes two 'limitations to the analogy': (a) Gentiles outnumbered Jews in the world and came to dominate the church and (b) being a Gentile is not an orientation.[25] There are, however, three more important theological divergences. First, the Gentiles are in a sense created by God in his salvation purposes as the other side of his election of Israel. Their identity is therefore inextricably tied up with the identity of God's people in a way that the gay

---

22 O'Donovan in Bradshaw, *The Way Forward?* p 24. One of the major advocates of this approach was, of course, Michael Vasey in *Strangers and Friends* and *Evangelical Christians and Gay Rights* (Grove Ethical booklet E 80).

23 This approach is misleadingly labeled homophobia. It is, as this analogy highlights, actually part of a more fundamental human and Christian failing and best labeled by a term opposite to that in current usage—hetero-phobia: fear of the other, fear of difference.

24 Siker, *Homosexuality in the Church*, pp 187, 189. His concluding comparison—'just as today most heterosexual Christians see active homosexuals as being sinners because they engage in homosexual activity'—is, however, unjustified.

25 *ibid*, pp 188–9.

identity is not. Secondly, the Gentile identity was constructed by Jews and was not the Gentiles' own identity. Whereas today someone tells us that they are gay and this is a category gay people have themselves discerned, defined and accepted, few first-century Gentiles would have understood themselves in terms of Jew/Gentile categories. Thirdly, leading into the next stage of the proposed analogy, God had always promised, from the creation of Israel in the call of Abraham (Gen 12), that the Gentile nations would be blessed through the Jews and had through the prophets spoken of their inclusion in his people. There is no separate, distinct promise for gay people. Rather, in the acceptance of Gentiles, there is already the full acceptance of all people and no sub-group or identity within humanity is therefore excluded from the grace of God in Christ.[26]

Although these dis-analogies should make us cautious about building too much on the Gentile-gay comparison, they do not destroy the significant parallels noted earlier. They may therefore weaken but they do not eliminate potential lessons from Acts 15.

2. Issue at Stake—Salvation and Status in God's People

The conflict in the early church which led to the Jerusalem Council had a clear and precise focus. Luke expresses it in v 1 and v 5 in terms of Gentiles needing to keep the law of Moses and in particular their need to be circumcised. Richard Bauckham sums up succinctly the fundamental theological, missiological and ecclesiological issues:

> The issue which divided the Jerusalem church at the time of the Council of Acts 15 was evidently not whether Gentiles could join the messianically renewed Israel, but whether they could do so without becoming Jews.[27]

Accepting, with some reservations, a possible analogy between Gentiles and gay people, the main issue Acts 15 might therefore help us resolve can now be defined. It is whether or not those who are homosexual can become Christians and full members of the body of Christ *as homosexuals*. If not it might be argued that they need wholly to renounce their homosexuality or even become heterosexual in order to be saved. To make Acts 15 the grounds for answering other questions in the current debate, while not impossible, requires much further justification.

---

26 The strong pattern of greater inclusivity in Scripture is not matched by a 'broadening' dynamic in relation to sexual conduct and relationships. In fact Christ and the apostles could be argued to move in the opposite direction with their teaching on lust and adultery (Mt 5.28), divorce and further marriage (Mk 10.1–12), and monogamy (1 Tim 3.3) countering parts of the Old Testament and reinforcing the witness of Gen 2. I am grateful to David Wenham for pointing out this contrast.
27 Richard Bauckham, 'James and the Gentiles (Acts 15.13–21)' in Ben Witherington III (ed), *History, Literature and Society in the Book of Acts* (Cambridge: CUP, 1996) p 168.

3. Solution

In Acts 15 the solution to the issue at stake is proposed by James. After summarizing what they have all heard he appeals to the prophets as in agreement with this account of the Holy Spirit's work. He cites Amos 9.11–12 in such a way as to allude to Hos 3.5, Jer 12.15 and Is 45.21 and insists that 'we should not trouble those Gentiles who are turning to God' (v 19).[28] Peter's plea, that to require full adherence to the law by Gentile converts would be to 'place on the neck of the disciples a yoke that neither our ancestors nor we have been able to bear' (v 10), has been heard and accepted. It is acknowledged that God has called and accepted them into his people *as Gentiles* and that the work of the Holy Spirit witnessed in their lives is evidence of this fact.

Mission, Inclusion and Transformation

Taking the analogy outlined above, a number of important implications for the current church attitude towards gay Christians can be drawn from this conclusion of the Jerusalem Council. These relate to what it means to preach the gospel to gay people and welcome them as gay people into the church. Three areas this touches upon are the mission of the church, the church's inclusivity, and the meaning of change.

First, the missiological implications. Just as Peter was challenged to take the difficult step of preaching the gospel across the major social and cultural barrier that existed between Jews and Gentiles, so the Christian church today must make the same, often difficult, step in relation to gay people. As in the early church, this has initially been done by a few brave individuals. They often received criticism from 'Bible-believing traditionalists' who saw it as a denial of an essential element of the church's identity, holiness and calling (the modern day form of Acts 11.2). Perhaps now the challenge is for Christian congregations not to leave this to isolated individuals and groups but to engage in such outreach themselves and so overcome common stereotypes of gay people.

Secondly, the ecclesiological implications. On the basis of the analogy from Acts 15 it must be insisted, against the objections of some, that 'gay Christian' is no more a self-contradiction than 'Gentile Christian.'

In the past many traditionalists have argued that homosexuality in any form is totally incompatible with Christian faith and discipleship. So, to quote one evangelical author in 1973, 'a church that decides to show compassion toward the homosexual by admitting him to full rights and privileges shows

---

28 The word translated 'trouble' suggests what we would term 'harassment,' again not an insignificant term for parallels with gay Christians.

a false compassion that confirms the sinner in his wicked ways.'[29] Although such attitudes remain in much of the church, this is beginning to change.[30] This happens as Christians take the pastoral challenges seriously, can testify to the work of the Holy Spirit in the lives of gay believers, and draw the conclusion that 'God, who knows the human heart, testified to them by giving them the Holy Spirit, just as he did to us, and in cleansing their hearts by faith he has made no distinction between them and us' (Acts 15.8–9).

Thirdly, the implications for change. Even where people have accepted that God has welcomed a lesbian or gay person and given them his Spirit, there is still often a view that they really need to become heterosexual and, in the title of a recent Channel 4 documentary, 'go straight.' The Gentile/Jew and Gay/Straight analogy is obviously weaker here but could perhaps be related to both gay identity and same-sex attraction.

At the level of identity this would mean that a gay identity need not necessarily be denounced and rejected any more than a Gentile identity had to be in the early church. That identity, however, like all human constructed identities, is now subordinated to our identity in Christ. This must be primary and foundational because, in the words of the St Andrew's Day Statement, 'Our sexual affections can no more define who we are than can our class, race or nationality.'[31]

As the gay identity is rooted in the experience of same-sex sexual attraction, there must also be a rejection of any insistence that 'healing' through prayer, counselling, or therapy is the best or only option for gay Christians. This view is still widely held by many 'traditionalists.' It holds that for the homosexual 'his restoration by God should eventually bring conformity to the creational order and a regaining of heterosexual desires. His final goal is God's ordained context and direction for sexual gratification—heterosexual marriage.'[32] The biblical evidence that among the changes God works in Christian lives includes making homosexuals into heterosexuals is highly tendentious (1 Cor 6.9–11 being the only possible reference). The scientific and anecdotal evidence for such complete and permanent reversals of sexual

---

29 Hal Lindsell in *Christianity Today* quoted in L R Holben, *What Christians Think About Homosexuality: Six Representative Viewpoints* (BIBAL Press, 1999) p 42. Similarly Bahnsen comments that it is 'plainly incorrect to hold that Scripture speaks only of homosexual acts...Paul holds men and women morally responsible and under God's wrath for burning with homosexual desires' (quoted *ibid*, p 37).

30 An example of this change is the recent Evangelical Alliance statement, *Faith, Hope and Homosexuality* (Carlisle: ACUTE/Paternoster, 1998).

31 As printed in Bradshaw, *The Way Forward?* p 7. This approach appears to be increasingly accepted across other divisions in the debate and marks an important development out of recent discussions. It criticizes not just some gay Christians but also those 'ex-gay' Christians and ministries claiming heterosexuality to be an important part of any person's true God-given identity.

32 Bahnsen, quoted in Holben, *op cit*, p 40.

orientation is minimal.[33] In this light there may well be a valid parallel from Acts 15. This would require the church to admit that in order to be full members in Christ's body gay people do not have to deny or seek to alter their attraction to people of the same sex. Whatever else may be required of them, they do not have to conform themselves to the heterosexual expectations which predominate in both church and society.[34]

In addition to these three possible implications of using Acts 15 in our current debate, a further and much more significant conclusion is drawn by 'revisionists' who currently propose the analogy. This argues that the church must also reject its traditional prohibition on all homosexual practice. It must not only welcome gay people but positively affirm homosexual relationships. So Siker views his argument as 'a case for seeing the acceptance of "non-abstaining" homosexual Christians as analogous to how early Jewish Christians accepted "non-abstaining" Gentile Christians.'[35]

Homosexual Practice and Relationships

Siker's 'revisionist' line of argument is also held to be valid by some evangelicals who object to drawing any analogies between Acts 15 and contemporary church debates. When Dick France appealed to Acts 15 in relation to the ordination of women, he was challenged that 'formally the arguments and methodology used by Dr France in his paper are exactly the same as those used for legitimating homosexual practice.'[36] There are therefore those on both sides of the current debate who seek to push for a choice: *either* use Acts 15 and accept homosexual relationships as the early church accepted Gentiles *or* reject homosexual relationships and refuse to use Acts 15 as a hermeneutical guide for current church controversies. This is in fact a false choice to force on the church. There are two reasons—one logical and one exegetical—why appeal to Acts 15 does not entail a 'revisionist' stance in the homosexuality debate.

First, Acts 15 is about accepting certain *people* within the church. This further supposed implication is about accepting certain *actions* of those people—patterns of behaviour and relationships. It is simply not possible to leap from one to the other. To do so would be the equivalent of saying that because one can see God's Spirit at work in a particular person's life or a

---

33 Some (significant) changes in sexual attractions do, of course, occur for some people and there is no need to deny this. However, even 'traditionalist' groups working with gay Christians are increasingly acknowledging that this is rare and some of their more grandiose claims have been false and highly damaging.

34 A recent 'traditionalist' discussion is Martin Hallett's 'Sexuality—A Gift From God?' at http://www.tftrust.u-net.com/testimony11.html.

35 Siker, *Homosexuality in the Church*, p 188.

36 Tinker, *Churchman*, Vol 108 No 3, p 246. For France's recent response see his *A Slippery Slope?* (Grove Biblical booklet B 16).

particular relationship there is no ground for passing a negative moral judgment on actions within that life. The church is, however, composed only and always of sinners. Those first Gentile converts, even when justified and Spirit-filled, all remained sinners. Just as the gift of God's Spirit to an abortionist, an active soldier or a wife-beating husband does not entail acceptance of every part of the social role and relationship through which they are being viewed, so the welcoming by God of gay people into the church does not necessarily entail the conclusion Siker and others have sought to draw. In other words, whilst one may be able to discern *whom* God accepts through the pattern of discernment evident in Acts 10–15, that process cannot tell *what* actions and relationships are acceptable to God as faithful Christian discipleship.[37]

Secondly, an even more serious objection can be made to revisionist appeals to Acts 15, based on the early church practice in relation to Gentiles. James affirms that Gentile believers should not be troubled but welcomed and accepted as Gentiles without having to become Jews. Nevertheless he then insists that they should abstain from certain things traditionally associated with Gentiles (v 20).[38] In itself these restrictions weaken the revisionist case and warn against pushing the analogy too far.[39] Even more seriously for this view, among the activities listed as prohibited is *porneia*. The exact meaning of this term is unclear but it is not impossible that it includes homosexual conduct.[40] This becomes even more likely when one understands the underlying rationale for the prohibitions insisted upon in the Apostolic Decree following the Jerusalem Council.

Although a number of proposals have been made as to why these four particular restraints were put on Gentile Christians, the most plausible is that James is again appealing to Scripture but without explicitly citing his authority. The most likely scriptural text is Leviticus 17 and 18 and Richard Bauckham has recently advanced a detailed supporting argument that reference to these chapters would correlate with the earlier citation of Amos

37 At Lambeth LGCM appealed not to have a yoke placed on them which it was impossible to bear. This was generally interpreted as drawing an analogy between circumcision and the demand that gay people abstain from sexual acts (*ie* enforced celibacy). Some gay Christians have, however, gone further and argued that marriage is a heterosexual requirement and that to impose it on gay sexual relationships is a refusal to let gay people be accepted as gay people. It is unclear how those who use Acts 15 to defend quasi-marital gay relationships can respond to this different application.

38 Debates about exactly what was decreed (due to textual variants and differences between v 20 and v 29) are not of importance for the point argued here.

39 Siker quotes comments of Stephen Fowl: 'The example of Acts 15 indicates that even though the Gentiles were included based on the recognition of their reception of the Spirit, they were also asked to observe certain practices that would enable table fellowship with Jewish Christians to continue. Would your argument recognize an analogous component?' (Siker, *Homosexuality in the Church*, p 194, n 16). See Fowl, *Engaging Scripture*, p 124.

40 Colin Brown, *Dictionary of New Testament Theology* (Exeter: Paternoster, 1976) 1:497ff. Richard Hays comments, 'the precise scope of the prohibited *porneia* is not explained in the story' (*Moral Vision*, p 383).

and allusions to other prophets. Bauckham argues that James is seeing the entrance of Gentiles *as Gentiles* into the people of God as their inclusion in the restored eschatological Temple. In the words of Jer 12.15–16 (alluded to in the promise of return in Acts 15.16a) the Gentiles are being built in the midst of God's people.[41] This then provides a link with Lev 17–18 which applies certain laws to 'the alien who sojourns in your midst.' In fact, Bauckham notes, 'the four things that are thus prohibited to "the alien who sojourns in your midst" correspond to the four prohibitions of the Apostolic Decree.'[42]

If this is the rationale underlying Acts 15 then the significance for its use in the current debates over homosexuality is revolutionary. The failure of 'revisionist' advocates to consider the limits placed on Gentiles by the Decree has always been a problem in their argument. The seriousness of that problem is now deepened if the Decree is based on Lev 17 and 18 and the prohibition of *porneia* therefore rooted in Lev 18.26. Among the 'detestable things' prohibited by that text are the male homosexual acts described in Lev 18.22.[43] There is now strong evidence that viewing homosexual practice as acceptable for gay Christians is not only to push the analogy from Acts 15 further than it logically can go. To make such a claim would in fact explicitly contradict one of the requirements placed on those Gentiles who entered the church as Gentiles.[44]

---

41 Bauckham, 'James and the Gentiles,' pp 163–4.
42 *ibid*, pp 172–3, referring to Lev 17.8, 10, 13 and 15 and Lev 18.26.
43 *ibid*, pp 173–4.
44 The continued significance of the Levitical prohibition has also been seen as underlying Paul's prohibition in 1 Cor 6.9 where the strange term *arsenekoitai* may have been coined from the Greek of Lev 18.22.

5
Conclusion—Where Can We Go from Acts 15?

The argument advanced here has been that Acts 15 can provide useful biblical guidance for how the church should respond to serious division over ethical matters. It has also been claimed that there are sufficiently close parallels that some analogies can be drawn for the specific ethical question of the church's relationship to gay Christians. In particular the evangelization of gay people and their inclusion on conversion into the body of Christ without any need to renounce their gay identity or reorient their sexuality could be said to follow from this analogy. However, Acts 15 has recently been proposed in order to suggest a biblically-based authorization for the church's affirmation of gay partnerships as commendable forms of Christian discipleship. Not only does this more important and far-reaching claim face the logical difficulty of pushing the analogy much too far, it also faces serious exegetical problems because Gentiles on entry into the church were expected to leave behind certain patterns of behaviour.[45] Acts 15 requests Gentiles to refrain from certain activities which were viewed as part of their Gentile identity and there is a strong case that amongst these was homosexual practice.[46] Far from being able to appeal to Acts 15 in a manner paralleling James' appeal to Amos 9, 'revisionist' appeals to this text are therefore equivalent to James citing as 'in agreement with' the welcome of non-circumcised Gentiles those biblical texts which speak of Gentiles having to be circumcised and obey the whole Law!

Is Acts 15 therefore unable to advance the 'revisionist' cause at all? Can this text only bolster a 'traditionalist' rejection of all homosexual conduct and further close down the current debate? Two alternative lines of argument may give a ray of hope to Siker and others wishing to press the Gentile/gay analogy but both advance nothing new and rely on other arguments 'revisionists' have already advanced.

First, the allusion to Lev 17 and 18 is not fully proven and the Decree may in fact be more limited in its *scope*. Ben Witherington's recent commentary presents an alternative rationale for the four prohibitions. This is based not a textual connection between them but a social one:

---

45 See Tim Bradshaw's 'Baptism and Inclusivity in the Church' in Stanley E Porter and Anthony R Cross (eds), *Baptism, the New Testament and the Church* (Sheffield, 1999) pp 447–66.
46 Hays remarks, 'If the prohibition of *porneia* in the apostolic decree (Acts 15.28–29) does include homosexual acts, that would be the one instance in the New Testament of a direct rule dealing with the issue. As we have seen, this reading of the passage is probable but not certain' (*Moral Vision,* p 394). In the light of Bauckham's study that reading is now highly probable.

The issue is…in what social setting one might find them together…The answer is likely to be in a temple…and in particular at a temple feast…Jews regularly thought such a combination of activities was likely by pagans in a temple…[47]

Thus, in relation to the crucial term *porneia*, Witherington limits it considerably in the Decree:

The term *porneia* in its most basic meaning refers to prostitution, including so-called sacred prostitution…*Porneia* is…precisely the right term to be used if James is thinking of the sort of thing that sometimes accompanied, or at least was believed to accompany, the pagan rites and feasts in pagan temples.[48]

On this interpretation, the only homosexual conduct Gentiles must refrain from is that in the context of idolatrous worship. If this can be held to apply here it may also apply to other New Testament prohibitive texts, notably Romans 1.[49]

Secondly, by limiting the Decree's *scope* in this way Witherington avoids the problem that otherwise elements of the Decree appear to have been limited in *time*. If what is condemned is limited to involvement in idolatrous sacrifice and cultic acts then the decree should clearly be applied universally to all Christian believers. If, however, the prohibitions apply in any and every context then a problem arises for the church has not insisted all the limits imposed are applicable in all times and places. Elements of the decree were not applied rigorously in all Gentile Christian communities and (given Paul's discussion in 1 Cor 8–10) this perhaps occurred quite soon after the Decree. It could therefore be claimed that the New Testament shows some elements of the decree, though necessary at the time of the Council, were later found not to be essential for the unity, purity and holiness of Christ's church. Here again the analogy may do some work for 'revisionist' readings. The argument would now be that, as with other elements of the Decree, so the apparently total condemnation of all homosexual conduct subsumed under *porneia* is open to reconsideration as the church welcomes and better understands gay people in same-sex relationships.

Even were one to grant this as a possibility, three further hurdles remain.

---

47 Ben Witherington III, *The Acts of the Apostles: A Socio-Rhetorical Commentary* (Michigan: Eerdmans, 1998) p 461.
48 *ibid*, p 463.
49 Interestingly, in tension with a standard 'traditionalist' rejection of limiting Paul's condemnations to cultic practice as historically implausible, Witherington claims it is 'frankly irrelevant how frequently such things actually did transpire in pagan temples' as what matters is that Jews believed they did occur (*ibid*, fn 421).

First, it would be rash in the extreme to believe the church as a whole is currently anywhere near ready to make such a judgment. Secondly, any such step is no longer based on an interpretation of Acts 15 as currently advocated. It has therefore to rely on other arguments in its support. Thirdly, the revisionist case still faces the difficulty that, unlike James in Jerusalem, it cannot argue its conclusions are supported or advocated by Scripture. Both the Old Testament and New Testament, although they contain negative statements about homosexual conduct, have no positive statement to which appeal can be made either directly or by analogy.

It is in this area—the prophetic witness of the church and her proclamation of truth—that 'revisionists' still face the greatest challenge. Their attempt to find a scriptural basis for changing the church's ethical stance on this issue through appeal to the narrative of Acts 15 has been shown to have value for the political task of maintaining the unity of the church during her ongoing discernment of God's will. Furthermore, in answer to the question raised at the end of section three—'What would it mean for the church to respond today to gay Christians as the early church did at Jerusalem in relation to Gentile Christians?'—elements of the church's attitude to gay people and some of its standard pastoral responses need to be challenged. Nevertheless, the value of Acts 15 for those seeking further to revise traditional church teaching on homosexuality is very limited. Indeed, by focusing attention on the Jerusalem Council, 'revisionists' may, ironically, have highlighted yet another biblical basis for insisting that, even as the church continues to struggle with this issue, to repent of its past hostility to gay people, and to welcome them into the church and learn from them as gay Christians, it must appeal to all disciples of Christ to refrain from homosexual conduct.[50]

---

50 'In our fallenness, brokenness, and confusion there is no place for rejection and lack of care for those intending discipleship, indeed the baptismal imperative challenges all cold judgmentalism: the church must urgently hear the challenge to develop ways of fostering meaningful fellowship and care for single people. Yet neither is there room for baptism itself to become a mark of endorsement of our patterns of worldly confusion instead of an entry into creative judgment on them and assurance of grace in facing them, in the fellowship of the church' (Bradshaw, 'Baptism and Inclusivity,' p 466).